Family Scrapbooking
Fun Projects to Do Together

Family Scrapbooking
Fun Projects to Do Together

Lael C. Furgeson

Stephanie F. Taylor

Sterling Publishing Co, Inc.,
New York
A Sterling/Chapelle Book

Chapelle Ltd.

Owner: Jo Packham

Editor: Linda Orton

Staff: Marie Barber, Ann Bear, Areta Bingham, Kass Burchett, Rebecca Christensen, Dana Durney, Marilyn Goff, Holly Hollingsworth, Susan Jorgensen, Barbara Milburn, Karmen Quinney, Leslie Ridenour, Cindy Stoeckl, Gina Swapp

Photography: Kevin Dilley, photographer for Hazen Photography

Designers: Lael C. Furgeson, Stephanie F. Taylor

Acknowledgements: A special thanks to the families of Nate and Connie Furgeson, Wyler and Denise Furgeson, Mark and Lisa Locklear, Deb Lovelidge, Erika Munns, Kevin and Dawnie Pickard, Simon and Barb Smith, and Sam Taylor for their time, energy, and numerous photographs.

Library of Congress Cataloging-in-Publication

Furgeson, Lael Combe.
    Family scrapbooking : fun projects to do together / Lael C. Furgeson, Stephanie F. Taylor.
       p. cm.
    ISBN 0-8069-2045-9
    1. Photograph albums. 2. Photographs--Conservation and restoration. 3. Scrapbooks. I. Taylor, Stephanie F. II. Title.
    TR465.F87 1999   99-39667
    745.593--dc21   CIP

10 9 8 7 6 5 4 3 2 1

A Sterling/Chapelle Book

Published by Sterling Publishing Company, Inc.
387 Park Avenue South, New York, NY 10016
© 2000 by Chapelle Ltd.
Distributed in Canada by Sterling Publishing
% Canadian Manda Group, One Atlantic Avenue, Suite 105
Toronto, Ontario, Canada M6K 3E7
Distributed in Great Britain and Europe by Cassell PLC
Wellington House, 125 Strand, London WC2R 0BB, England
Distributed in Australia by Capricorn Link (Australia) Pty Ltd.
P.O. Box 6651, Baulkham Hills, Business Centre, NSW 2153, Australia
Printed in China
All Rights Reserved

Sterling ISBN 0-8069-2045-9

If you have any questions or comments, please contact:

Chapelle Ltd., Inc.
P.O. Box 9252
Ogden, UT 84409

Phone: (801) 621-2777
FAX: (801) 621-2788
e-mail: Chapelle@aol.com

Lael Furgeson has been interested in art since she was a child and developed it more fully through advanced education. Her interest in layout design was put to use while operating a very successful Interior Design firm in California. After moving to Boston, Massachusetts, and later on to Jackson, Mississippi, Lael became involved in designing high-end clothing art for three well-known fabric paint manufacturers. She authored six instructional books on designs and techniques for clothing art. After returning to California, she co-authored a book on doll house furnishings.

Family Scrapbooking allowed Lael the experience to design and co-author with her daughter Stephanie. Stephanie's desire since childhood to collect memorabilia and keep journals made her a "natural" for co-authoring a "how-to" scrapbook. Lael enjoyed the experience of putting their heads together and being on such a creative high while completing this book in Stephanie's Paris, France, home, leaving her with many fond memories.

I must thank my very patient husband for going along with my "dreams and endeavors", not to mention the supplies I "must" have to support them. He is a gem and I appreciate his good nature all of these years. A special thanks to Stephanie's husband for his help when we needed time to collect our thoughts and create scrapbook pages while on the other side of the world. An additional and loving thanks to Stephanie's small children who were more than patient. We could not have undertaken this project without all of their support.

As a young girl growing up in San Jose, California, Stephanie Furgeson Taylor worked in her mother Lael's interior design studio. Stephanie observed her mother's love of working with fabrics, accessories, and furniture and marveled at how her mom could make a room come alive. After working in Boston as a court reporter for several years, Stephanie decided to follow those creative impulses inspired by her mother and embarked on a new career in creative scrapbook design when she moved to Valencia, California. There Stephanie began teaching classes at scrapbooking and craft stores, which led to becoming an in-house designer for a leading manufacturer of scrapbooking papers and supplies. Dozens of her early designs have been published in scrapbooking magazines and books. In the summer of 1998, international flavor was added to her scrapbook designs when the Taylor family moved to Paris, France. It was in Paris, shortly after the birth of her second daughter, where Stephanie and her mom created the memory pages for this book.

First and foremost, this book is dedicated to my mother, my greatest source of inspiration, who led me to explore my own creative talents and helped me take a chance to make my dreams come true. It is also dedicated to my two darling daughters, Ashton and Céline, who are the joy of my life and provide me with the required motivation as I try to capture their individual personalities upon scrapbook pages. And lastly, to my wonderful husband Sam, who offers support and encouragement, even when portions of our home look like the aftermath of a scrapbooking shop hit by a tornado.

Table of Contents

Chapter One

Chapter Two

Introduction

The main objective of *Family Scrapbooking* is to show you how to have a rewarding experience with scrapbooking to preserve your memories. There are so many of us that have photos stashed away in a drawer or closet, and how often do we ask questions such as "How old was she?" or "When did we live in that particular home?" These details become difficult to remember when photos are set aside too long. Creating scrapbook pages is a great way to record details and family memories.

The Basic Idea of Family Scrapbooking

Family Scrapbooking invites all members of the family to participate in the scrapbooking process. This is a different approach from many other publications today which are primarily targeted to "mom." Exciting scrapbook ideas and pages are included that can involve the children, dad, and the grandparents as well. Ordinarily, dad does not even dream that he could be included in putting together scrapbook pages with the children. It may surprise everyone—especially him—that he could enjoy the experience.

The primary idea is to create wonderful scrapbook pages made by family members. "Annual Cookie Making" portrays a family tradition and engages grandmother and the grandchildren in designing and making a scrapbook page that is complete with warm memories.

"Collage Fun" and "Connor" are just two examples of scrapbook pages that can be easily made and are fun to do with children. "Connor" consists of mosaic art done with small colored squares cut from paper scraps and includes children as young as four years of age. Having plenty of supplies on hand is the key for keeping a child's attention and focus on a project. Family scrapbooking can be lots of fun!

Where to Begin?

Scrapbooking can be a unifying family activity, accomplished not from pressure and guilt, but with the desire to preserve wonderful memories. Scrapbooks will mean even more to family members when they have been included in the process.

For some families, time is a limitation, so you may wish to select scrapbook pages that require less time and fewer supplies. Scrapbook pages may be simple or elaborate, it is all up to you.

This book has been divided into chapters allowing you to select the amount of time and supplies available to assemble a great page. The chapters vary from simple and quick pages with theme page ideas for family involvement to economical pages, getting more from less, using odds and ends to the more advanced pages.

To begin, go through the photos that you already have and place them into groups that you would like to use on a page. It is best to begin with your most recent photos and work back from there. This applies to your scrapbook pages as well, since the memories and details will be fresher than those of years past. Some groupings may not have many photos, so those will automatically have a more simplified layout. Other stacks may contain a number of photos on the same subject, but it is good to have a number of selections from which to choose. You can do photo organization while relaxing in the evenings. Use the large size resealable plastic bags—which may be reused—by placing each page's subject or theme in a bag with a slip of paper identifying it. It is amazing how many photos you can get through in just a few evenings. When you have some time to put a page together, all you have to do is select a bag that has already been separated.

If there is more than one child in the family and you want to do an album for each child, simply color copy the completed page, place in a plastic page protector, and insert into other scrapbooks. This way you will not be so overwhelmed when having to make multiple pages.

Getting started is the most difficult part, but once you and the family are involved in scrapbooking, a lifetime of memories are recorded and important ties are created from one generation to the next.

Scrapbooking In General

Webster's dictionary defines the scrapbook as "a blank book in which miscellaneous items are collected and preserved." In the last few years, preserving to keep or save photos and memorabilia from decomposition has taken on new meaning with the popularity of scrapbooking. So many of us have keepsakes which have been passed down from one generation to the next, and we want to be able to pass these down to yet another generation. Scrapbooking can be a significant tribute to those who came before us. What is a better way than to preserve the memories and stories in album form, to tell future generations what the world held for us in our day as well as those before us? Historical roots in scrapbook form can be a wonderful gift to family members.

In order to preserve these keepsakes, photos, and papers from decomposing, archival professionals have found that there are certain steps we can take to save these treasured memories and ensure that our books will last for generations.

Archival

When you are putting so much time and energy into a scrapbook you will want it to be around for many years to come. If this is the case, you will want to make certain that all materials and supplies are archival quality. In the case of papers, you will want to purchase papers that are acid-free and lignin-free. For glues and pens, always purchase those that also are acid-free. Read labels to make certain that any products you purchase—from papers and stickers, to pens and adhesives—are archival. Acid-free adhesives, papers, pens, stickers, and other supplies are readily available at scrapbook and craft stores. If you are uncertain whether a product is acid-free, you can call the manufacturer's customer service.

Acid is an unstable chemical that causes photos and papers to bleed, fade, and deteriorate over time. An object contains acid if it has a pH of 7.0 or less. If you are not certain

whether or not a paper is acid-free, a pH-test pen may be purchased to check the acid content in papers.

Keep in mind that even though a product is acid-free, it may not stay that way because of acid migration from high-acid products in close proximity, environmental pollutants, or oils from human hands to acid-free products.

Buffered papers are acid-free and acid-absorbent. Many scrapbookers will use buffered papers at the beginning and end of their scrapbooks to protect the contents from acid migration.

Occasionally, you may want to add a piece of memorabilia that contains acid to your

scrapbook. There are a couple of options available: 1) you can photocopy the memorabilia on acid-free paper, 2) purchase a buffering spray that neutralizes acid in the paper and adds a protective coating, or 3) place it in a protective page cover.

To be truly archival, photographs should be removable, which means that removable adhesive or photo corners are best for mounting photos. Store unused photos and negatives in archival boxes or files in a dry place away from the sun.

If you have any photos that have been placed in self-adhesive albums, you will want to remove them at once. The adhesive contains the chemical polyvinyl chloride (PVC), which is destructive to photographs. The photos fade, become brittle, and become difficult to remove over time. If your photos are difficult to remove, try using a cake spatula or dental floss to lift them from the page. If your photos cannot be removed with a spatula or dental floss, try using a blow dryer set on medium to soften the gum adhesive. If photos are still not removable, you may want to take them to be color copied.

When you make your scrapbooks using archival products, they will be there for future generations to enjoy and treasure. You may pay a little more for archival products, but they will be worth it over the years.

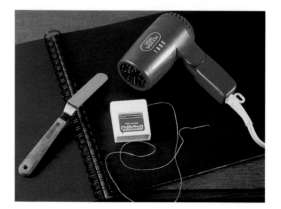

Speaking of Supplies...

Scrapbook Sizes

Sizes vary from very small to quite large with the most popular being 8½" x 11", to 12" x 12", and 12" x 15". Some information to keep in mind regarding the various sizes are:

1) 8½" x 11"—Because of the smaller page size, you are limited to a smaller size and number of photos that may be placed on the page. However, the availability and large assortment of papers, quick page completion, storage in three-ring binders, and a lowered cost are just a few of the benefits in using this size for scrapbooking.

2) 12" x 12"—This is a specialty size that can be purchased at scrapbook stores or at scrapbook parties. They are more expensive to purchase and the availability and assortment of papers are more limited. The benefits to this size are that more photos will fit on a page and some albums are expandable to hold more pages.

3) 12" x 15"—This is another specialty size album that can be purchased at scrapbook stores or scrapbook parties. Generally, they are the most expensive size, but if you take a lot of photos, these albums would probably be a good choice for your needs. Another drawback is that you will probably need to piece sheets of paper or card stock together for the page background.

The various scrapbook pages in the following chapters are designed in the 8½" x 11" or 12" x 12" formats. Keep in mind that you may use any scrapbook page instructions for either size with some minor layout adjustments.

Other Scrapbook Supplies of Importance

Adhesives:
Adhesives come in several forms and you should use only those that are acid-free.

- *Double-sided segmented tape* is easy to use and was designed for mounting photos, but works well for die-cuts and other page accents.
- *Glue sticks* are inexpensive to use and a good choice where children are involved in scrapbook page layout. Glue sticks work best on photos and paper page accents.
- *Glue pens* with a fine point are used for small areas where a glue stick or tapes are too wide for application.
- *Double-sided tape runner* is similar to the segmented tape, but is a continuous piece that can be torn off at the desired length.
- *Self-adhesive foam dots* are another choice if you want your designs to have dimension and stand out from the paper. One of the drawbacks to dimensional design is that the raised surfaces can leave impressions on other pages.

The adhesive that you choose to use will depend on the materials and layout for your pages and designs as well as your personal preference. Most of the scrapbook pages in this book can be made with a glue stick unless a specific adhesive is recommended.

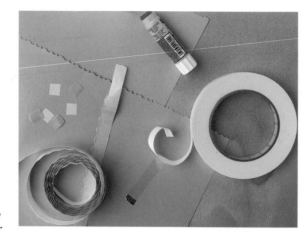

Album pages, papers, and card stock:
These are the types of papers that will be used for background, matting, and decoration on a scrapbook page. It is important that all papers and pages used in an album are acid-free and lignin-free if you intend to keep photos and other items from decomposing.

Circular blade paper cutter:
For a perfectly straight cut, the paper cutter will probably be of more use than any other tool for scrapbooking. This paper cutter has a round blade, which is pulled from the top to the bottom of a photo or paper for a precise cut. The cutting blade and straightedge are attached to a ruled surface, making it very easy for measuring. Ripple or other decorative-edged blades are available for some of these paper cutters. Discount stores will have the best prices and it will be money well spent because it saves so much time.

Corner clipping scissors:
These scissors are used for making decorative designs on paper corners.

Corner punches:
These are designed to punch decorative edges on corners of papers and card stock.

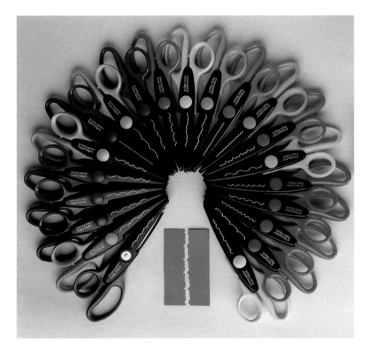

Novelty-edged rulers:

These come in handy when you want precise trimming on a border or elsewhere. There are rulers available with a different design on each edge of the ruler, which is two for the price of one. Patterns come in different styles, such as scallops, zigzags, and many more.

Page protectors:

These are clear sleeves into which a finished page can be slipped for protection with holes punched on the side so they can be placed into an album. Some open from the top while others open on the side. Read the package to verify that they are acid-free. For scrapbook pages that will be handled often, these sleeves offer an invaluable protection.

Decorative-edged scissors:

These scissors are used for cutting decorative edges on paper and card stock for photo and page accents. You will find many designs to choose from. At first, you may want to try those of a fellow scrapbooker. Then you can acquire a few of the designs that you like best.

Die-cuts:

These are punched-out designs and usually come in the heavier paper or card stock weight so they do not bend in narrow areas. A number of shapes, designs, and words are available. At many scrapbook stores, you can have them punched out in a custom color or type of paper.

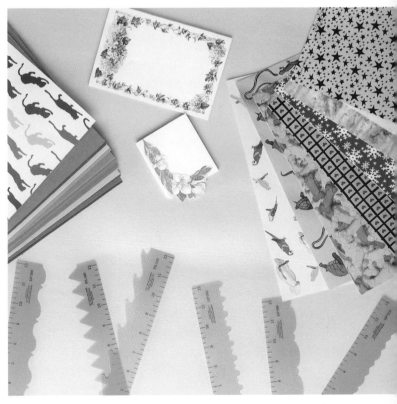

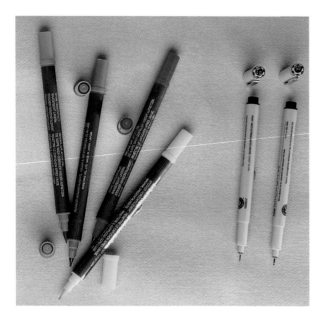

Pens, pencils, and markers:
There are many pens and markers to choose from, varying in purpose and width of point. They should be pigment ink, acid-free, fade-proof, and waterproof.

- A *journaling pen* has a fine-point tip (0.5 mm) and is used for writing under photos and labeling.
- *Markers* are used for lettering on pages or doing background designs around photos. A marker with a scroll tip can add variety to a page, providing a perfect parallel line or design work on page borders or around photos.
- A *brush marker* is great for enhancing around photos and on backgrounds.
- There are various types of *calligraphy pens* that come in an array of colors and point sizes. These are used for titling pages.
- The *dual-tipped "fine* and *chisel" markers* are also good for lettering in various sizes—from small captioning with the fine-point tip to large headers with the wider felt tip.
- *Metallic pens* of gold and silver are a must for every scrapbooker's collection.

Just a stroke of a metallic pen on certain pages gives enough sparkle to add that finishing touch.

- A *white opaque pen* is fabulous on dark papers, great fun to experiment with, and will give a whole new look to a page. The opaque pens also come in other colors that you will want to try.
- A *photo-safe pencil* is specifically designed for labeling photos. You can also use it to trace a template onto the photo surface without damaging it.

Our advice to beginners is that it may be best to buy a package of pens or markers in assorted basic colors and add specialty colors and types as desired.

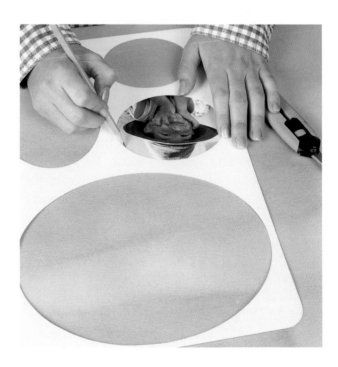

Plastic template pages: Templates are manufactured from a stiff plastic and are ordinarily 8½" by 11" in size. Templates are available in circles, ovals, squares, frames, and numerous other theme shapes in various sizes that have been machine-cut to give a firm edge to trace around.

Punches:

These are used to punch out small designs and can be found in a number of designs and sizes. A single punch, such as a heart, can be turned into flowers or bugs. One of the best features about punches is that you can use the punched-out shape as well as the void area by trimming around it, like we did with the Mickey Mouse punches on page 98.

Solid and patterned papers:

The solid papers come in every color imaginable, including tints, shades, and tones of gray. Metallics, heathers, glossies, pearl finish, and patterned papers are also available, plus too many more to list.

Sticker lettering:

These are great to use when you are still trying to master hand-lettering on scrapbook pages. We have used these letters in a variety of sizes and colors throughout our book, because of their ease.

Stickers:

There is a wide array of stickers available in segments or packages, which include hobbies, talents, florals, pets, strips, and page accents, or just about everything else you can imagine. The manufacturer should state on the sticker segment or package if they are acid-free; if not noted, they probably are not.

Transparent ruler:

This is a quilters' ruler that is 4" wide x 12" long, with ⅛" to 1" markings and can be purchased in a fabric or quilt supply shop. Because it is transparent, it allows you to line up your layout perfectly. It is particularly handy for lining up lettering.

Where to Start With Supplies...

If you are on a budget and want to start with the basics, our suggestion would be to purchase the following supplies:

- **Adhesives:** glue stick; segmented tape in plastic dispenser
- **Marker:** black, medium-point for titles
- **Page protectors**
- **Papers and card stock:** neutral colors for background; several colors for accents and matting photos
- **Pen:** black, fine-point for journaling
- **Photo-safe pencil**
- **Plastic template pages:** circles; ovals

- **Sticker lettering:** black, medium, upper-/lowercase
- **Stickers:** bright dots; $\frac{1}{8}$"-wide bright strips; or a few designs in black and white

When your budget permits, add the following supplies so that you have a few more choices:

- **Die-cuts:** family or personal hobbies and sports; words
- **Markers or pens:** set of colors
- **Patterned papers:** holiday motifs; heathers; polka dots; or stripes, whatever suits your circumstances

- **Plastic template page:** squares
- **Straightedge cutting tool**

The following items can be added as you have the need for them:

- **Stickers:** general, to be used on a variety of subjects
- **Decorative-edged and corner clipping scissors**
- **Metallic pens**
- **Novelty-edged rulers**
- **Punches:** general designs, such as an apple, circle, heart, and sun
- **Sticker lettering:** colored letters or metallic

Some Additional Tips for Scrapbooking

Technical Tips:

1) Save any scraps of papers, so when a page calls for a bit of color, you can use scraps rather than purchasing or cutting up whole new sheets. Slip your scraps into large mailing envelopes and label as solids, prints, or other descriptions. Whenever you want to add a bit of color or punch out designs, such as autumn leaves, you can go to your scrap envelope for a variety of whatever color scraps are needed.

2) Place photo scraps in another large mailing envelope and label it. For a different approach, you can trace lettering on the photo scraps, cut out, and mount them on a scrapbook page for a title with patterned letters.

Design Tips:

1) When purchasing punches, select those that can be used in multiple ways, such as a heart for flowers, valentines, or split it to make a ladybug, leaves, or whatever else you may think of. Many of the punches can be used in this manner.

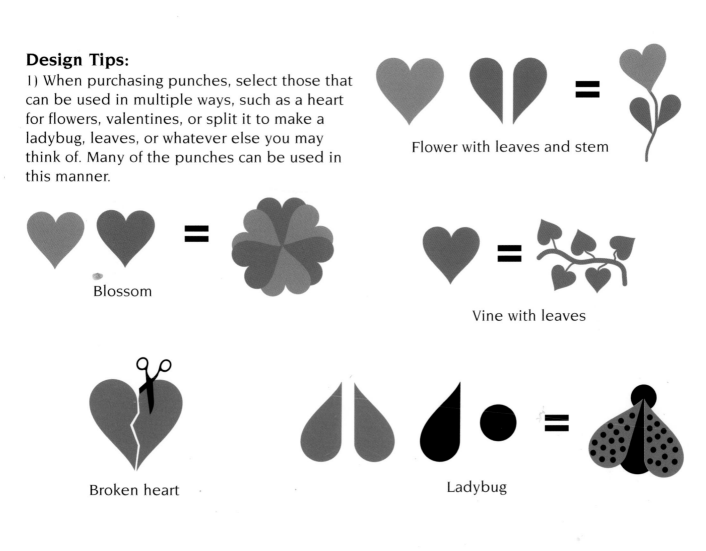

Flower with leaves and stem

Blossom

Vine with leaves

Broken heart

Ladybug

2) When using punches, such as a star, use the star which was punched as well as the piece from which the star was punched by cutting around it with decorative-edged scissors. Try punching along an edge of the paper, creating a border.

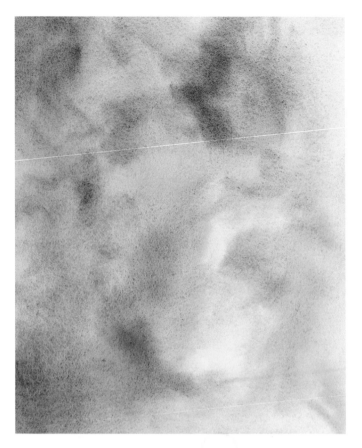

3) Watercolor on a piece of watercolor paper or card stock with bright colors or pastel washes. This page makes an attractive background.

4) Pens may be used to make decorative free-hand borders around photos and backgrounds. It is a good idea to practice on a separate sheet of paper before drawing the borders on your scrapbook page.

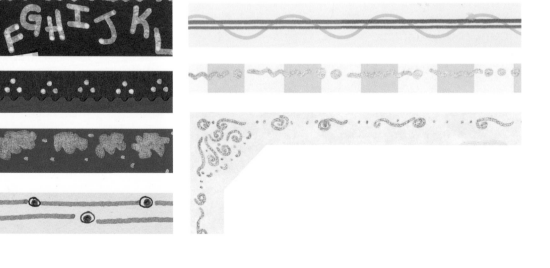

Photography

Preserving memories begins with capturing experiences on film and placing them in a collective order. The more scrapbooking you do, the better photographer you will become. You will be more aware of what you need for the page and be better prepared to capture quality action. Those spontaneous photos that say this is an unforgettable moment will be more creative, as will your arranged shots become better backgrounded. It is worth it to get a second set of prints developed. Some stores may give you two sets for the price of one. This allows you to do pages for two albums if desired, or if mistakes are made, a second photo is available. Watch newspaper ads for sales on developing. Additionally, you may use a color copier for extra copies, or for enlarging or reducing photos.

Composition will become better as you become more aware of the elements in your photos when you begin to place them on a scrapbook page. Like any skill, practice will make you a better photographer. Stand close enough to your subject to see their eyes and details of what they are doing. Stand closer to your subject to get more in the viewfinder, cutting out a lot of blank space in front. Tall subjects look better if the camera is held vertically, so that you are able to take in all of your subject. Groups should be taken horizontally unless they are placed stair-stepped.

If you have a red-eye problem on your photos, there is a pen available to correct red-eye at most scrapbook stores. The pen is applied directly to the photo and it contains a dye that filters out the red and allows the natural color to show through.

Cropping Photos

When cropping photos for layout, look at photos and determine what the main action of the photo is. Many times there is too much background or foreground and it can be trimmed off. If you choose to crop your photos, it will make the subjects appear closer by trimming off some of the foreground. Also, this will allow you to place more photos on the page to tell the story.

Vignetting is another cropping approach for photos. It means that you trim around your subject, following their contours. Vignetting is not for every page or photo, sometimes the background setting is as important as the primary subject is to the page. Take your time and use a small pair of scissors with a slender blade so that you can cut around corners and delicate areas, such as hands. Be particularly careful when you cut around hair so that you do not make the subject look as though their head is misshapen by taking off too little or too much hair.

Creating Decorative Mats for Photos

Most photos look better when surrounded with a tiny bit of color or decoration. Matting is a simple thing to do and with some experimentation you will create wonderful mats that accent your photo and enhance the entire scrapbook page. There are just a few simple steps to take into consideration when matting your photos:

1) Determine how you wish to crop your photo. If using a template, trace shape onto photo using a photo-safe pencil.

2) Select an archival paper or card stock that is complementary to your photo and page background.

3) Cut paper to be used for matting larger than your photo and glue photo onto paper.

• Cut mat large enough so a design can be drawn around the edge of your photo with a marker or pen.

• Patterned papers can be as attractive as solid papers.

• Mat a round photo on a square mat or try a silhouetted photo on an oval mat.

• Use a corner punch to make decorative corners on your mat.

• Double- or triple-mat your photos with other complementary colors.

Decorative mat ideas:

• Use decorative-edged scissors to cut mat and give it an instant decorated edge. You can cut all four edges with decorative-edged scissors or just one, two or three sides.

Tip: When selecting a paper for matting, you may want to lay your photos on top of several colors of papers you think will enhance your photos, then select the best choice.

Chapter One

Family Scrapbooking Fun

The scrapbook page ideas in this chapter are ideal for children and their creativity.

Punches, torn edges, and school pictures, along with lots of art supplies is the way to involve the younger family members.

Theme page idea:
Take photos of the children while they are "collaging." Have them make extra collaged pages without photos so that you can place new photos of each child on their very own page.

Cut out lots of different-sized circles, rectangles, squares, squiggles, strips, and triangles from various bright-colored scraps. This gives everyone a variety of choices. If a white background is used, the possibilities for color combinations are unlimited. Glue the white card stock onto a bright background for a splash of color.

- White and yellow card stock for background:
  1. Cut white card stock smaller than yellow and glue onto yellow.

- Circle template • Bright-colored solid and patterned paper scraps:
  1. Cut out a variety of shapes.
  2. Trace several circles and cut out.
  3. Glue shapes and circles onto background in collage, reserving a few to overlap onto photos.

- Photos:
  1. Crop photos as desired and glue photos onto background.

- Green lowercase sticker lettering:
  1. Place lettering on individual paper shapes and glue shapes onto background.

collage fun

25

SCRAPBOOK PARTY WITH DADDY

This page will be priceless because of dad's involvement. It will work best with a variety of supplies, such as colored papers and stickers. These are the types of supplies that dad and the children can easily use.

★ White card stock (2) for backgrounds
  • Removable tape:
    1. Lay card stock side by side and tape together on the back side.

★ ⅛"-wide bright-colored strip stickers:
    1. Place one sticker ¼" from edges of backgrounds.

SCRAP BOOK

★ Bright-colored solid papers:
  1. Cut strips of paper in varying widths and glue onto backgrounds. *Option: Cut curvy edge on one side of strip for variation.*

★ Circle and oval templates • Photo-safe pencil • Photos:
  1. Trace circles and ovals onto some photos and crop.
  2. Crop remaining photos as squares, rectangles, and vignettes.
  3. Glue photos onto background.

★ Black, uppercase sticker lettering
  • Bright-colored circle stickers:
  1. Place lettering on background.
  2. Place stickers on background as desired.
  3. Remove tape from background and cut down center between pages, separating any art that is glued onto both backgrounds.

Tip: Use photos whose subject matter is "dad with the children" for this project.

Theme page idea: Take photos of the children and dad doing scrapbook pages. This will make a great project for the next time dad and the children make scrapbook pages together.

WE LOVE TO DO ART PROJECTS AT GRANDMA'S

Theme page idea: Take photos of the children while they are being creative and use the same supplies on the new scrapbook page that they were using in the photos.

Young children love any involvement with the adults in their family. The key to doing this page with children is the inclusion of many supplies, such as origami folding paper in great colors, watercolored tissue, colored dots, and artwork stickers. Children are creative and will do amazing projects with provided art supplies.

▲ Pink card stock for background

▲ Photos:
   1. Crop photos as desired.

▲ Decorative-edged scissors • Origami and tissue papers:
   1. Cut paper slightly larger than photos. *Option: Tear one edge and cut remaining edges.*
   2. Glue photos onto paper. *Note: If papers are not acid-free, they may need to be sprayed with buffering spray before gluing photos.*
   3. Glue photos and paper onto background.

▲ Colorful markers • Stickers • Colored papers:
   1. Decorate background as desired.

▲ Black uppercase sticker lettering:
   1. Place lettering on page.

WE LOVE TO DO

ART

PROJECTS AT GRANDMAS

BY Camille

Tip: Allowing the words to be spread throughout the page adds interest and makes excellent use of space.

Connor

The rainbow background is an artwork project that children will enjoy working on. Use current photos of the child and have them write their name and age on a piece of paper to include on the scrapbook page.

■ White card stock (2) for background •
Removable tape:
1. Lay card stock side by side and tape together on the back side.

■ ⅛"-wide blue and yellow strip stickers:
1. Cut strips at a diagonal ½" to 1" shorter than length of page.
2. Place strips as shown on scrapbook pages.

■ Solid paper scraps in rainbow colors:
1. Cut ½" squares in a variety of colors and glue onto backgrounds, creating a mosaic rainbow. *Option: If* *younger children are working on this page, you may want to cut the squares in advance.*

■ White card stock • Blue marker:
1. Have child write name and age.
2. Cut out name and age.

Photos:
   1. Crop photos as desired.

Blue/white polka-dot, blue/white stripe, and yellow/blue geometric patterned papers:
   1. Cut papers in various shapes for matting photos, name, and age.
   2. Glue photos, name, and age onto shapes. *Option: Double- and triple-mat some of the photos.*
   3. Glue photos, name, and age onto background.
   4. Remove tape from background and cut down center between pages, separating any art that is glued onto both backgrounds.

Theme page idea: Create mosaic theme designs that would go along with a photo, such as an ocean made from cloud and blue shades of papers, for a family beach trip.

Tip:
When doing a two-page layout, remember not to place any important elements that will be cut and separated, such as the middle of your subject's face.

KEVIN, MATTHEW, AND DADDY

Tip: Crop photos large and use two to three so that background can be seen and the page will not be too busy.

This is a quick and simple, yet attractive page, using the leaf patterned paper for the background. There is no need for a punch or additional papers for this page, making it quite economical.

✦ Autumn leaf patterned paper for background

✦ Circle and oval templates
  • Photo-safe pencil
  • Photos:
   1. Trace circles and ovals onto photos and crop.
   2. Glue photos onto background.

✦ Yellow uppercase sticker lettering:
  1. Place lettering on background.

so many choices

This is an easy page to make and an excellent opportunity to use some of your paper scraps. Children will want to help make this page. They love to tear the paper pieces and punch out the pumpkins and leaves.

▼ Pale gold card stock for background

▼ Green plaid and green with dots patterned papers:
  1. Tear out six to seven irregular shapes from papers.
  2. Tear one long strip from green with dots paper.
  3. Glue strip onto bottom of background.

▼ Photos:
  1. Crop photos as desired.

▼ Metallic gold paper:
  1. Cut paper slightly larger than photos and glue photos onto paper.
  2. Glue photos and remaining torn shapes onto background. *Option: Tuck some edges of torn shapes under photos, and allow other edges to overlap onto photos.*

▼ Apple punch • Dk. gold, orange, and peach paper scraps:
  1. Punch seventeen apples for pumpkins and glue onto background.

▼ Small oak leaf punch • Green paper:
  1. Punch seven leaves and glue onto background.

▼ Green lowercase sticker lettering:
  1. Place lettering on page.

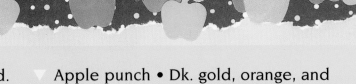

Spencer's Artwork

BY Spencer
age 9

Children love to draw when they are young. Give them supplies and let them draw to their heart's content. Remember to have them sign their "masterpieces" and write their age on a separate piece of card stock. Their writing and how old they were at the time will be looked upon as a treasure when they are older.

- Red and white card stock for background:
    1. Cut white card stock smaller than red card stock. Glue white card stock onto red card stock.

- Bright-colored markers • White card stock:
    1. Have child create artwork; write name and age.
    2. Cut around artwork, name, and age. Glue onto background.

- Photos • Photo-safe pencil • Oval template:
    1. Trace an oval onto one photo and crop.
    2. Crop remaining photos in squares and rectangles.

- Green leaf and yellow/white checkered patterned papers:
    1. Cut leaf paper slightly larger than photos and glue photos onto paper.
    2. Cut checkered paper ⅜" larger than name and age. Glue name and age onto paper.
    3. Glue photos and name onto background. *Option: A photo could be double-matted with checkered paper to add interest.*

- Rainbow and various-sized iridescent dot stickers:
    1. Place stickers on background as desired.

A tie-dyed style background, music and brightly patterned papers, sticker lettering, and gold stars show off this budding musician following in grandpa's footsteps.

OFF TO SCHOOL!

Maternelle "Roule"

Kevin Age 3

Neuilly-sur-Seine, FR

9 2 '96

OFF TO SCHOOL

Going off to school is certainly a day to remember, along with a backpack that weighs almost as much as the child. This is a good layout if you are short on time and it may be used for a variety of subjects.

✎ Alphabet patterned paper for background

✎ Photo:
  1. Crop photo as desired.

✎ "Off To School" patterned paper:
  1. Cut out title.

✎ Corner punch • Green and yellow paper:
  1. Cut green paper ¾" larger than photo and punch corners.
  2. Cut green paper ¼" larger than "Off To School." Glue "Off To School" onto green paper.
  3. Cut yellow paper ¼" larger than photo. Glue photo onto yellow paper and double-mat onto green paper.

✎ Black marker • School supplies, ¼"-wide alphabet strip and theme book strip stickers:
  1. Place alphabet strip down right side of background.
  2. Place school supplies stickers around photo. Glue photo and "Off To School" onto background.
  3. Write child's name, age, school, and city on theme book strip and place on background.

AGE 5

KELVIN

Tip: Having the child write their name and age allows
them to see their development over the years.

KEVIN

Each school year, children bring home packets containing school pictures. This is a great opportunity to use one photo for each year and place it in a scrapbook of achievements. Down the road, they will look through this book and cherish the chronicled years.

Tip: You will want the child's face and personality to be the emphasis here. When selecting the background, choose a subdued and rich color. Take a close look at the photo and see what the dominant colors are. We chose a pine green in a deep rich tone. The brick color was selected because it is subdued in tone. Forest green and gold were selected to use with the pine green and brick colors, and to add additional interest.

Pine green card stock for background

★ Individual school photo:
   1. Crop off white border from photo.

⅛"- wide metallic gold strip stickers:
   1. Cut two strips at an angle with one slightly longer than the other.
   2. Place strips down right side of background.

★ Black marker • Brick-colored paper:
   1. Have child write name and age on paper. Cut out name and age.
   2. Cut brick paper ¼" larger than photo and glue photo to paper.

Decorative-edged scissors • Forest green card stock • Metallic gold medium-point pen:
   1. Cut card stock ¼" larger than brick-colored paper and photo.
   2. Randomly dot card stock and glue to background.

★ Metallic gold paper:
   1. Cut paper slightly larger than name and age. Glue name and age onto paper.
   2. Glue name, age, and photo onto background.

Chapter Two

Quick and Economical

When time and money are limited, here are some ideas that will allow you to create price-less scrapbook pages.

Although you may have different subject matters than those presented, you can adapt any of these pages to your particular theme.

You will have photos that need a very special scrapbook page, such as this one of the grandchildren. Look for a dominant color which appears in several places in the photo to make your paper and lettering choices.

◆ Black card stock for background

◇ Photo:
   1. Crop photo as desired.

◆ Black with dots, red/white polka-dot, and red/white striped patterned papers:
   1. Cut black paper ¼" larger than photo and glue photo onto paper.
   2. Cut polka-dot paper larger than black.

3. Cut striped paper larger than polka-dot.
4. Glue striped paper, polka-dot paper, and photo onto background as shown on scrapbook page.

◇ Opaque red pen • ⅛"-wide red strip and ⅛"-wide black/white strip stickers
• Decorative sticker lettering:
   1. Draw a dotted line border around outside of striped paper.
   2. Place strips on background.
   3. Place lettering on background.

Baby ★ Taylor
October 5ᵀᴴ
★ 5 lbs. 2oz.
★ Paris

TWINKLE TWINKLE LITTLE STAR HOW I WONDER WHAT YOU ARE UP ABOVE THE WORLD SO HIGH LIKE A DIAMOND IN THE SKY

TWINKLE TWINKLE LITTLE STAR

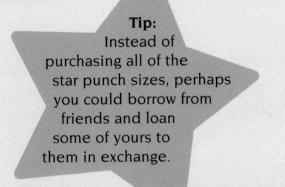

Tip:
Instead of purchasing all of the star punch sizes, perhaps you could borrow from friends and loan some of yours to them in exchange.

A nursery rhyme inspired this layout to use a precious baby photo which becomes the "star" on this page. Use a photo of the baby lying peacefully that can be cradled in the moon. This photo was enlarged in order for it to be the right proportion.

★ Purple with stars patterned paper for background

★ Photo:
  1. Vignette photo.

★ Matte metallic silver paper • Moon Pattern:
  1. Enlarge Moon Pattern 200% and photocopy onto white card stock.
  2. Cut out moon and place on silver paper. Trace moon onto paper and cut out. Set scraps aside to use for punching stars.
  3. Glue moon and baby onto background.

★ Large, medium, and small star punches:
  1. Punch stars from silver paper scraps and glue onto background.

★ Opaque metallic silver medium-point pen:
  1. Write baby's name, birth date, birth weight on background.
  2. Add any quotes, such as "Twinkle twinkle little star . . ." under the moon.

Moon
Pattern

Enlarge 200%

ANNUAL COOKIE PARTY

Annual Cookie Party

When putting together a page such as this, shoot lots of step-by-step action photos during the process, such as mixing the ingredients, baking the cookies, and all the rest of the fun children have right up to licking the bowl! To get all of the steps on the page, some photos were vignetted, which allowed space for the baking stickers. Use your imagination on this type of scrapbook page, since children like to be in the kitchen cooking hot dogs, grilling hamburgers, popping popcorn, making candy, or anything else involving one another and doing something fun.

- Cream card stock for background

- Photos:
  1. Crop photos as desired and glue photos onto background.

- Red/white polka-dot patterned paper:
  1. Cut one 1" strip of paper and glue strip onto top of background.

- Black and blue uppercase sticker lettering:
  1. Place lettering on background, mixing letter colors.

- Baking-themed stickers:
  1. Place stickers on background.

that's what friends are for!

Use a number of photos on this scrapbook page, show some of the background, and note locations on the map. A favorite phrase for this group of friends and the title for this page is "that's what friends are for.

◆ Map patterned paper or color copy of map for background

◆ Photos:
　1. Crop photos as desired. Glue photos onto background, allowing some photos to extend off edge of paper.
　2. Trim off edges that extend beyond background.

◆ Iridescent star stickers:
　1. Place stars on map background to pinpoint places where friends in the photos live.

◆ ⅛"-wide red strip stickers:
　1. Place strips around edge of background.

◆ Green lowercase sticker lettering
　• Red wide-tip marker:
　1. Place lettering on background.
　2. Outline words as shown on scrapbook page.

Tip: If the photos are too small, enlarge them by making color copies.

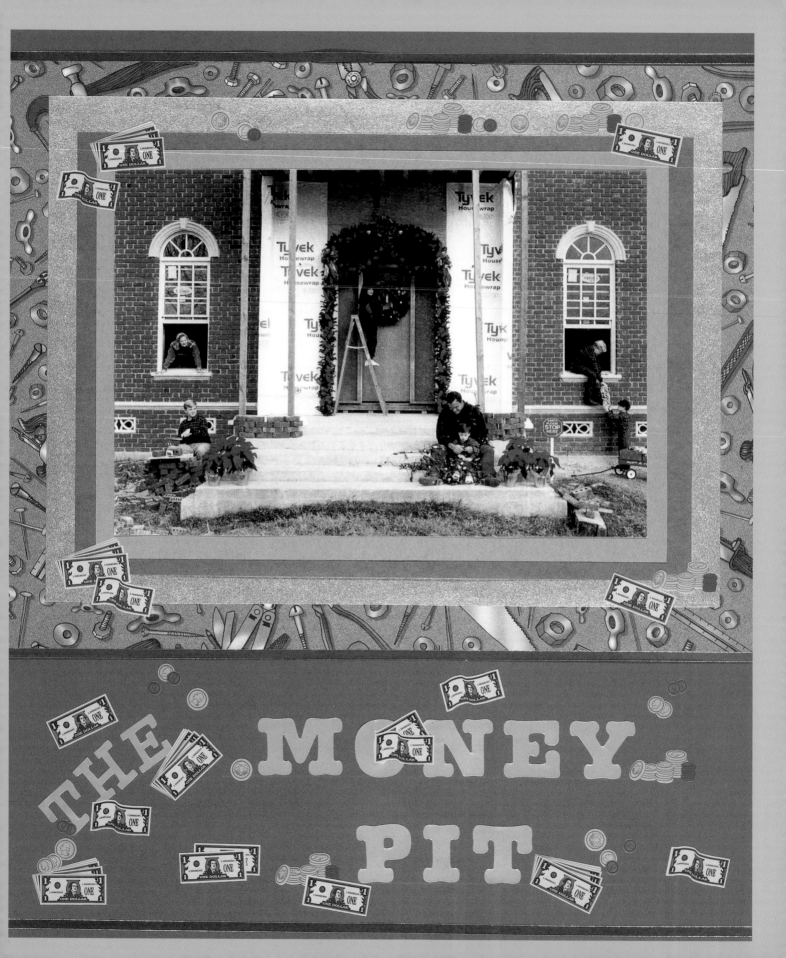

THE MONEY PIT

The Money Pit

This was a fun page to design. The photo was taken for the family's Christmas card, which was sent to family and friends. The photo is triple-matted in different colors to make it stand out. A patterned theme paper with tools was selected because it related to the building of a home. It is one of those quick and easy pages you might be looking to do.

▼ Cinnamon card stock for background

▼ Photo:
1. Crop photo as desired.

▼ Camel, green, and silver papers:
1. Cut camel paper larger than photo and glue photo onto paper.
2. Cut green paper larger than camel paper and double-mat photo onto green paper.
3. Cut silver paper larger than green paper and triple-mat photo onto silver paper.

▼ Tool patterned paper:
1. Cut paper, if necessary, to fit width of background, allowing same size margin on top and bottom of triple-matted photo.

    2. Glue paper and photo onto background.

▼ ⅛"-wide metallic copper strip stickers:
1. Place strips as shown on scrapbook page.

▼ Metallic silver uppercase sticker lettering (2 sizes):
1. Place lettering on background.

▼ Paper money and coins stickers:
1. Place stickers on background.

Ballet
&
Tap
class

Ballet & Tap Class

If your child has a particular interest or hobby, such as an art class, dancing class, gymnastics, Scouts, 4-H, or other, take a camera to class and start shooting from the beginning of the class to the end. You will have a story photographed in picture form. This makes a great page and a memory your child will never forget.

♥ Pink card stock for background

♥ ⅛"- silver metallic strip stickers:
   1. Place strips on background as shown in scrapbook page.

♥ Circle and oval templates • Photo-safe pencil • Photos:
   1. Trace circles and ovals onto some photos and crop.
   2. Crop remaining photos into rectangles.
   3. Glue photos onto background.

♥ Pink/white polka-dot upper- and lowercase sticker lettering • Iridescent hearts and ballet shoes stickers:
   1. Place lettering, hearts, and ballet shoes on background.

♥ Black medium-point and cranberry fine-point markers:
   1. Draw black dots under letters and shoes to give the hint of a shadow as shown on scrapbook page.
   2. Draw cranberry zigzag border around photos.

IT'S TIME TO HAVE A BABY

Of course, not in the dogs' eyes, since they will definitely slip down the ladder in importance! This is another quick page for a busy family. This page consists of enlarging and color copying a photo, double-matting it, and adding some stickers.

- Dog bone patterned paper for background

- Photo or enlarged color copy:
    1. Crop photo as desired.

- Black and tan papers:
    1. Cut black paper larger than photo and glue photo onto paper.
    2. Cut tan paper larger than black paper and double-mat photo onto paper.
    3. Glue photo onto background.

- Dog accessory stickers:
    1. Place stickers on black paper.

- Black uppercase adhesive lettering:
    1. Place lettering on background.

IT'S TIME TO HAVE A BABY

Napa
&
Sonoma

If you go into a well-stocked scrapbook store, you will see unbelievable choices of paper colors, not only the solid shades, metallics, and glossies, but also patterned papers of heathers, theme motifs, and much more. A grape-colored solid paper was used for this background since it was fitting to the subject of vineyards.

> **Tip:** Sometimes it is difficult to determine what shade of paper you will want to use with a photo or group of photos. Line up several colors on the table and lay photos from the same grouping on top of each color to see which colors look best with the photos. Keep in mind when you are at the scrapbook store to look for wonderful colors, even the unusual, because at some point in time, you will probably find a need for that special color or pattern purchased six months ago.

✦ Grape card stock for background

✦ Photos:
  1. Crop photos as desired and glue photos onto background.

✦ Decorative-edged scissors • Light plum mulberry patterned paper:
  1. Cut two photo corners for each photo with decorative inside edge as shown on scrapbook page.
  2. Glue photo corners onto photos.

✦ Fleur-de-lis punch • Matte metallic gold paper:
  1. Punch nine fleurs-de-lis and glue onto background.

✦ Gold upper- and lowercase sticker lettering:
  1. Place lettering on background.

Napa &
Sonoma

Merry Christmas!

KISSING BOOTH

Christmas Kissing Booth

This is a family Christmas Card and it makes a great page in a scrapbook. Glue the photo onto a background and you have spent little time because it is just about complete with a little extra embellishment. Scrap pieces, such as the matte silver, come in handy so you do not have to buy a whole sheet.

- Red card stock • Red/black plaid patterned paper for background:
    1. Cut plaid paper smaller than card stock and glue onto card stock.

- Matte metallic silver paper:
    1. Cut rectangle from paper and glue rectangle onto background.

- Photo:
    1. Crop photo as desired and glue photo onto plaid paper.

- "Merry Christmas," holly, gift, and kiss stickers:
    1. Place "Merry Christmas" on silver paper.
    2. Place remaining stickers on background.

Chapter Three

More for Less

These pages look like lots of supplies were needed, but, they use simple design techniques and materials and create such wonderful scrapbook pages. The key is to keep the layouts simple and get more out of your scrapbook supplies whether it is in making your own patterns and cut-outs in place of die-cuts or combining stickers that you already have on hand.

helping Daddy

Raking up and then playing in the piles of leaves is a fun activity to do each fall. Dad had as much fun falling in the leaf piles as the boys did. This is a great page for children and dad to make together.

Tip: When cropping photos, determine the most interesting part of the photo, place the template, and trace.

◆ Wood patterned paper for background

◆ Geometric shapes template • Photo-safe pencil • Photos:
   1. Trace geometric shapes onto photos and crop.
   2. Glue photos onto background.

◆ Maple and oak leaf punches • Gold, greens, oranges, tan, and yellow paper scraps:
   1. Punch a variety of leaves and glue onto photos and background.

◆ Green upper- and lowercase sticker lettering:
   1. Place lettering on background.

helping

Daddy

MOMMIE'S LIL ANGELS RASCALS

Matthew
NO GIRLS!
KEVIN
KIDS ONLY!
daddy's tools
COMICS

Tip: There are so many great stickers, keep an inventory on hand from which to select. The stickers used on this page were from several different manufacturers and worked well together.

Mommie's Li'l Rascals

You will have pictures like this one, which are priceless and do not come along very often. This was the perfect story to try out some unique stickers that had been collected. The boys look like they are thinking about squirting the dog, building a tree house, scaring the cat, playing with snails and jumping frogs, walkie-talkies, flashlights, and whatever else goes with a summer play day.

Tip: Be creative, try weaving stickers in and out or setting them on top of the letters.

Blue card stock for background

◆ Oval template • Photo-safe pencil • Photo:
  1. Trace an oval onto photo and crop.

◆ Oval template • Green, red, and yellow papers:
  1. Cut a green oval slightly larger than photo and glue photo onto oval.
  2. Cut yellow rectangle larger than oval and double-mat photo onto yellow rectangle.
  3. Cut red rectangle larger than yellow and triple-mat photo onto red rectangle.
  4. Glue photo onto background.

◆ Red uppercase sticker lettering:
  1. Place lettering on background.

◆ Miscellaneous stickers:
  1. Place stickers on background.

RACHEL

This is a simple page to make, yet it looks like a lot of time went into it. This page is successful because of the dynamic contrast of color. This child was dressed in bright pink, setting the color theme for the scrapbook page.

Tip: Keep in mind when you are photographing children that when their clothing is bright, it looks like lots of fun is happening.

■ Hot pink card stock for background

■ Photo:
  1. Crop photo as desired.

■ Decorative-edged scissors
  • Black and white card stock
  • Black uppercase sticker lettering:
  1. Cut white card stock slightly larger than photo with decorative edge.Glue photo onto card stock.
  2. Cut white card stock into rectangles with decorative edge, large enough for lettering. Place lettering on card stock.

3. Cut black card stock slightly larger than photo and white card stock. Double-mat photo onto card stock.
4. Cut black card stock slightly larger than letter rectangles and double-mat lettering.
5. Glue photos and lettering onto background.

■ ⅛"-wide black strip and music-themed stickers:
  1. Place strips diagonally on upper right corner of background.
  2. Place stickers on background.

OUR FIRST SNOWFALL

Our First Snowfall

This is a "more with less" page. It was done with just a few supplies, and tells a story that a child can recall as a fun day in the snow with friends. Photos were taken of the group as well as the individual children.

✳ Snowflake patterned paper for background

✳ Photos:
    1. Crop photo as desired.

✳ Decorative-edged scissors • Cloud patterned and white papers:
    1. Cut white paper with decorative edge on bottom larger than photos and glue photos onto paper.
    2. Cut blue paper with decorative edge on bottom larger than white paper and double-mat photos onto blue paper. Save scraps for snowflakes.
    3. Glue photos onto background.

Tip: Remember to take individual pictures at group activities. Give yourself as many choices as possible when shooting photos.

✳ $\frac{1}{8}$"-wide metallic silver strip stickers:
    1. Place strips across bottom of photos.

✳ Large and small snowflake punches • Cream, silver, and white paper scraps:
    1. Punch a variety of snowflakes and glue onto background.

✳ White uppercase sticker lettering:
    1. Place lettering on background.

RIVER

VOLLEYBALL

There are times when family fun is hard to coordinate and get everyone together for a vacation, camping, or reunions. So, if for no other reason than that, you should be taking the camera along and shooting lots of photos of all those involved and the activities going on. This page is a great layout for any outdoors, woodsy scrapbook page.

▲ Camping patterned paper for background

▲ Photo:
   1. Crop photo as desired.

▲ Brown plaid patterned, brown, lt. green, and med. green papers • Tree Patterns:
   1. Cut two 2¼"-wide strips from plaid paper. Glue strips at an angle onto background paper as shown on scrapbook page. Trim excess paper from background edges.
   2. Cut med. green paper larger than photo and glue photo onto paper.
   3. Cut brown paper larger than green paper and photo, and double-mat photo onto brown paper.
   4. Glue photo onto background.
   5. Enlarge Tree Patterns 200% and photocopy onto card stock for patterns. Cut out trees.
   6. Trace one small and one large tree onto med. green paper and cut out.
   7. Trace one large tree onto lt. green paper and cut out.
   8. Glue trees onto background.

▲ Brown uppercase sticker lettering:
   1. Place lettering on background.

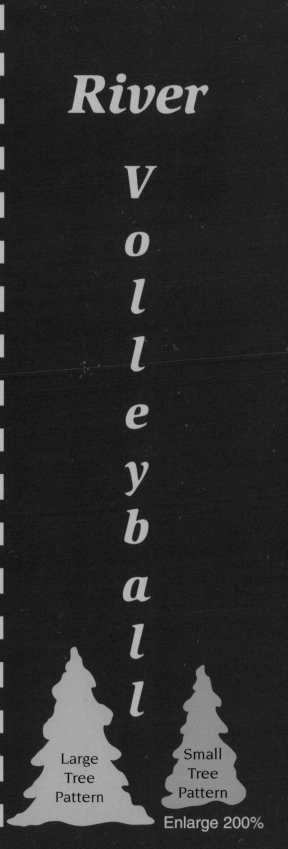

River Volleyball

Large Tree Pattern

Small Tree Pattern

Enlarge 200%

MEET ME AT THE TOP

Living in a city of parks is the perfect excuse to toss the camera into the backpack when going cycling. With a helping hand and the click of a shutter, everyone was in the shot recording a family play day.

Meet Me At The Top

Tip: Consider titling the scrapbook page, using a statement that goes with what is happening in the photo.

- Contemporary orange/gold plaid patterned paper for background

- Vertical view photo:
    1. Crop photo as desired.

- Pale gold parchment paper:
    1. Cut paper larger than photo and glue photo onto paper.
    2. Glue photo onto background.

- Gold and orange papers • White uppercase sticker lettering:
    1. Cut gold paper in rectangles larger than individual letters.Place letters on rectangles.
    2. Cut orange paper larger than gold and double-mat letters onto orange paper. Glue lettering onto background in a tumbling effect.

IRELAND

When you think of Ireland, you automatically think of green. This young college student went to Ireland with friends and has done enough scrapbooking to understand that saving everything makes for a more interesting story. She brought home bus passes, an airplane ticket stub, and receipts from the hotels. The pictures are great, from the sheep's back ends to the rock coming down from above.

◆ Green plaid patterned paper (2) for background • Removable transparent tape:
  1. Lay card stock side by side and tape together on the back side.

◆ Photos:
  1. Crop photos as desired.

◆ Checkered and green/white polka-dot patterned papers • Lt. green parchment paper:
  1. Cut papers larger than photos and glue photos onto papers.

◆ Ticket stubs, receipts, brochures, or other travel mementos:
  1. Glue photos and travel mementos onto backgrounds.

Note: *Allow some of the background pattern to show between pictures.*

◆ Green uppercase sticker lettering • Lt. pink and green parchment papers:
  1. Cut out rectangles larger than lettering from pink parchment. Place lettering on rectangles.
  2. Cut green parchment larger than pink and double-mat lettering onto green parchment. Glue lettering onto background.
  3. Remove tape from backgrounds and cut down center between pages, separating any elements glued onto backgrounds.

IRELAND

EASTER, EASTER, EASTER

This holiday scrapbook page has a panoramic photo view across the top of the page which shows the expanse of the crowd waiting for the Easter Egg Hunt. Combine the panoramic photo with six oval-shaped photos and the story is told in pictures.

Tip: Create your own water-color background page. Refer to *Design Tip #3* on page 20.

♦ Pastel watercolor-style paper for background

♦ Panoramic photos • Photo-safe tape:
   1. Match smaller photos carefully to make one long photo.
   2. Tape photos together on back side.
   3. Crop top and bottom of photos so they are long and narrow.
   4. Glue photos onto background.

Tip: If you do not have a panoramic camera, you may use your regular camera. Stand at a distance from the panoramic view that you wish to photograph. Photograph at the same level, taking three to four shots by moving the camera horizontally, but not vertically.

♦ Oval template • Photo-safe pencil • Photos:
   1. Trace ovals onto photos and crop. Glue photos onto background.

♦ ⅛"-wide pastel strip and bow stickers:
   1. Place strip across top edge of panoramic photo.
   2. Place bow at an angle on strip.
   3. Place strip along bottom edge of background.

♦ Bunny, duckling, and egg stickers:
   1. Cut one egg in half with jagged edges. Place egg pieces over duckling as if it is hatching.
   2. Place remaining stickers on background.

♦ Gold uppercase sticker lettering:
   1. Place lettering on page.

Theme page idea: Try the panoramic photo idea with other subjects, such as at a soccer or football game, or other gatherings where there are large groups at a distance.

EASTER

EASTER

DIPLOMA

GRADUATION

Graduation

Here is another quick and easy page layout which uses few supplies and turns out quite nicely. It is a clean and masculine design, as well as an effective scrapbook page. This layout will work with many different themes.

★ Army green card stock for background

★ Photos:
    1. Crop photos as desired.

★ Graduation patterned and rust papers:
    1. Cut 5¾"-wide strip from graduation paper. Glue strip at an angle onto background and trim excess from edges.
    2. Cut four ⅛"-wide strips from rust paper. Glue strips at an angle onto background as shown on scrapbook page.

★ Beige parchment paper:
    1. Cut parchment ¼" larger than photos and glue photos onto paper.
    2. Glue photos onto background.

★ Graduation cap die-cuts • Graduation stickers:
    1. Place stickers and glue die-cuts onto background.

★ Black uppercase adhesive lettering:
    1. Place lettering on background. *Note: You may want to place year of graduation on background.*

Family
Christmas Card

If you send out photo Christmas cards, a scrapbook is a great way to keep track of them. The photo on this page was cropped on the diagonal as an oval in order to take in more of the sleigh's detail.

Tip: Keep an eye out at scrapbook or copy stores for unusual papers. Watch out year round for unusual seasonal papers, such as Christmas, Easter, birthday, or other.

◆ Red card stock for background

◆ Christmas patterned paper:
  1. Trim around details such as the bow.
  Option: Paper can be cut into two pieces, as was done with this paper. Ribbons were matched up and an attractive backing was created on which to glue photo.

◆ Oval template • Photo-safe pencil
  • Photo:
  1. Trace an oval onto photo and crop. Glue photo onto Christmas paper.

◆ Opaque gold metallic medium-point marker:
  1. Make squiggly motifs around border of background and around photo.
  2. Randomly dot around motifs.
  3. Glue photo and paper onto background.

◆ Metallic gold uppercase sticker lettering
  • Holly stickers:
  1. Place lettering on background.
  2. Place stickers on background.

Family Christmas Card 1998

Chapter Four

Odds and Ends

The following scrapbook pages will take you beyond the store-bought supplies look. Many of the materials are of a unique nature. These pages may take a bit more time because of the extra page accents, but even a beginner can make these by following the step-by-step instructions.

Take photos of a child in one of their favorite outfits against a background that complements their clothing. If a child is particularly fond of school, you could use a school theme, complete with stickers and plaids, to suggest a "back to school" look. Play up the single photo by double-matting the photo with solid colors. Letters are placed on apple stickers to further reflect the school theme.

✎ Red/white small plaid patterned paper for background

✎ Red/white large plaid patterned and red papers:
   1. Cut 1¾"-wide strip from plaid paper and glue strip onto left side of background.
   2. Cut 1"-wide strip from red paper and glue strip along center of plaid strip.

✎ Photo:
   1. Crop photo as desired.

- Crayon patterned, red, and white papers:
    1. Cut white paper ¼" larger than photo and glue photo onto white paper.
    2. Cut red paper ¼" larger than white paper and double-mat photo onto red paper.
    3. Cut crayon paper ¾" larger than red paper. Glue crayon paper onto the back-ground at an angle. Trim edge even with page if necessary.
    4. Glue photo onto crayon paper.

- Apple stickers • Black uppercase sticker lettering:
    1. Place individual letters on apples.
    2. Place apples on background.

- Crayon and school-themed stickers:
    1. Place stickers on background.

Butterflies
Are
Fun

© 1994 THE PAPER COMPANY E-490-A   © 1994 THE PAPER COMPANY E-490-A

Butterflies Are Fun

Butterflies, bugs, and other creatures fascinate children, which allows for some great photo-taking opportunities. The background paper with the beautiful butterfly border on one side is perfect for this layout. All you will need are a couple of contrasting patterned papers and an extra sheet of butterfly paper.

♥ Butterfly bordered paper for background

♥ Circle and oval templates • Photo-safe pencil • Photos:
   1. Trace circle onto one photo and crop.
   2. Trace oval onto one photo and crop.
   3. Crop remaining photos as desired.

♥ Decorative-edged scissors • Orange patterned and yellow papers:
   1. Cut yellow paper slightly larger than circle and oval photos. Glue photo onto paper.
   2. Cut orange paper larger than remaining photos with decorative edge on three sides.
   3. Cut orange paper slightly larger than circle photo and double-mat photo onto paper.

   Silhouetted photos, bright background, fun bug stickers laminated in a cut-out jar, and a loose-weave fabric cut for a butterfly net complete this unforgettable scrapbook page.

♥ Butterfly bordered paper • Sunflower stickers • Decorative sticker lettering:
   1. Cut out three butterflies.
   2. Glue butterflies and photos onto background.
   3. Place lettering and sunflowers on background.

Tulips and Daffodils

The yellow background and a sunny spring day with flowers as far as the eye can see, makes this bright scrapbook page a family treasure. The upper center photo was cropped long and narrow to look like a panoramic photo. Some photos were vignetted, while others were enlarged and color copied to better see facial expressions.

✦ Yellow card stock (2) for background • Removable tape:
  1. Lay card stock side by side and tape together on the back side.

✦ Decorative-edged scissors • Oval template • Photos • Red paper:
  1. Enlarge and color copy two photos. Trace ovals onto color copies and cut out.
  2. Cut two ovals slightly larger than photos and glue photos onto paper.
  3. Crop one landscape photo with decorative edge on top.
  4. Crop remaining photos as desired.
  5. Glue photos onto backgrounds.

✦ Floral wreath, leaf, and strip stickers:
  1. Place stickers on backgrounds, using some to frame photos.

◆ Green upper- and lowercase sticker lettering:
   1. Place lettering on background.
   2. Remove tape from backgrounds and cut down center between background pages, separating any art that is glued onto both backgrounds.

◆ Opaque gold metallic medium-point pen (optional):
   1. Draw dot designs on backgrounds.

Tip: You can add extra template sizes to your library by tracing an existing template onto a sheet of paper, enlarging it 50% and copying onto card stock. Cut out the ovals, using a craft knife. You can use the openings or the ovals as your templates.

SHARK ENCOUNTER

WE ALL HAD

HARBOR

A GREAT DAY!

A Great Day!

Sometimes you have a group of pictures that are not terribly exciting. It may have been an overcast day and the color in the photos are dull, but this is when stickers, lettering, and paper color comes into play, along with a little creativity on your part. Lay out the photos and see if there is a single color which trickles through all the pictures. This will help to determine a pleasant background to play up the pictures. In this case, the theme was determined, the stickers along with the rope detail were added, and a successful scrapbook page was completed.

▼ Aqua card stock for background

▼ Oval template • Photo-safe pencil • Photos:
   1. Trace ovals onto photos and crop.

▼ Decorative-edged scissors • Gold paper:
   1. Cut rectangles larger than two photos with a decorative edge on one edge. Glue photos onto rectangles.
   2. Glue all photos onto background.

▼ Royal blue uppercase sticker lettering
   • Ship-themed stickers:
   1. Place lettering and stickers on background.

▼ White or cream embroidery floss:
   1. Pierce background for rope.
   2. Cut three equal pieces of floss.
   3. Knot one end of floss pieces together.
   4. Thread floss in and out of pierced background, knotting at intervals. Knot remaining end to secure.

CELEBRATE

★CELEBRATE

Look through the photos that you have taken to see if there is a great single picture that you can play up with balloons. Maybe it is a special birthday, anniversary, homecoming celebration, or simply a happy photo.

★ Matte silver paper for background

★ Photo:
   1. Crop photo as desired.

★ Metallic red paper:
   1. Cut paper ¼" larger than photo and glue photo onto paper.

★ Decorative-edged scissors • Metallic blue paper:
   1. Cut blue paper ½" larger than red paper, and double-mat photo onto blue paper.

★ Metallic blue, red, and glossy white card stock • Balloon Pattern:
   1. Cut red card stock ½" to ¾" larger than blue paper and photo. Glue red card stock onto background.
   2. Glue photo onto red card stock on background.
   3. Photocopy Balloon Pattern onto white card stock and cut out.
   4. Trace three balloons onto each color of card stock and cut out.

★ Hologram silver stars:
   1. Place stars on background as desired.

★ Self-adhesive foam dots
   • Red and gray embroidery flosses:
   1. Place one side of dot on wrong side of balloons. Place balloons on background as desired.
   2. Cut six pieces of gray floss in varying lengths to fit the placement of the balloons. Glue one end of floss under each balloon. Allow to dry.
   3. Pull ends of balloons together, wrap and knot with red floss. Glue in place.

★ Red uppercase sticker lettering:
   1. Place lettering on background.

Balloon Pattern

Cinderella

This scrapbook page includes some items which are not really what you would think of when scrapbooking comes to mind. Fairy tale character postage stamps found their way into the scrapbook supplies. A favorite fairy tale, starring the child, makes an adorable "happily ever after" scrapbook page.

♥ Blue gray card stock and moiré patterned paper for background:
   1. Cut moiré paper smaller than card stock and glue moiré paper onto card stock.

♥ Oval template • Photo-safe pencil • Photo:
   1. Trace an oval onto photo and crop.

♥ Decorative-edged scissors • Lt. blue paper • Theme postage stamps:
   1. Cut oval with decorative edge slightly larger than photo and glue photo onto paper.

2. Cut paper slightly larger than stamps and glue stamps onto paper. *Note: One stamp could be double-matted onto a contrasting color scrap.*
3. Glue photo and stamps onto background.

♥ Silver uppercase sticker lettering:
   1. Place lettering on background.

♥ Hologram makeup and heart stickers:
   1. Place stickers on background.

THIS SPACE MAY BE USED FOR
CORRESPONDENCE

*When you are
married & living
at ease
Remember one
who loves to tease*

*many Happy
Xmases to you
and Daddy &
Kiddies —*

HAPPY
VALENTINES
DAY

Happy Valentine's Day

A romantic page where the photo is enhanced by an oval silver mat glued onto a rectangle of black. Place the picture on an angle, add handwritten notes, die-cut hearts, and rose stickers, and a scrapbook page worthy of the Victorian era is created.

Tip: Whether drawing borders, lettering, or decorative motifs, first practice on a separate sheet of paper until you get a feel for what you want to do.

✦ Red moiré patterned paper for background

✦ Oval template • Photo-safe pencil • Photo:
  1. Trace an oval onto photo and crop.

✦ Old letter patterned paper:
  1. Cut paper into separate letter pieces and glue pieces onto background. Save one piece to overlap onto photo.

✦ Black card stock • Matte silver paper:
  1. Cut paper in an oval ⅛" larger than photo and glue photo onto paper.
  2. Cut card stock rectangle larger than photo and double-mat photo onto card stock.

3. Glue photo onto background at an angle. Trim any mat edges that run off background edges.

✦ Die-cut hearts • Silver hearts and Victorian rose stickers:
  1. Cut through left side of white heart.
  2. Link hearts together as shown on scrapbook page and glue onto background.
  3. Place stickers on background.

✦ Black dual-tipped pen • Silver upper-case sticker lettering:
  1. Draw swirl motif on background and place lettering on motif.

Putting on TIGGER

Tigger

Tigger

PUTTING ON TIGGER

Which was more fun—putting on the costume, face painting, or assembling the scrapbook page? Capturing a night to remember for a memory collection is what you want scrapbooking to be all about. If you achieve this, that is the end goal for a successful scrapbook page.

■ Candy corn on white patterned paper for background

■ Circle and oval templates • Photo-safe pencil • Photos:
  1. Trace a circle onto one photo and crop.
  2. Trace ovals onto some photos and crop.
  3. Crop remaining photos as desired.

■ Black/orange checkered patterned, orange, and yellow papers:
  1. Cut square larger than circle photo from black/orange checkered paper. Glue photo onto paper.
  2. Cut yellow and orange papers slightly larger than remaining photos. Glue photos onto papers. Note: A wavy edge may be cut around edge for oval photos.
  3. Glue photos onto background.

■ Orange uppercase sticker lettering • Candy corn patterned and yellow papers:
  1. Cut yellow paper into squares larger than letters. Place letters on squares at angles.
  2. Cut candy corn paper slightly larger than yellow paper. Double-mat yellow paper onto candy corn paper as shown on scrapbook page.
  3. Glue lettering onto background.

■ ⅛"-wide yellow/orange checkered strip stickers:
  1. Place strips on top and bottom of background.

E♥M♥I♥L♥Y

Here is a great theme page to play up the importance of a child's musical endeavors. A page of sheet music cut smaller than the green background and each corner embellished with a decorative corner punch creates a page celebrating the individual.

- Green card stock and music patterned paper for background • Decorative corner punch:
  1. Trim paper on an angle smaller than card stock.
  2. Punch corners of paper and glue onto card stock.

- Photo:
  1. Crop photo as desired.

- Decorative-edged scissors • Black and tan papers:
  1. Cut tan paper slightly larger than photo and glue photo onto paper.
  2. Cut black paper with a decorative edge larger than tan paper and double-mat photo onto black paper.
  3. Glue photo onto background.

- Decorative-edged scissors • Medium and small heart

punches • Music patterned, black, green, red, and tan paper scraps • Vase Pattern:
  1. Enlarge 200 % and photocopy Vase Pattern onto white card stock and cut out.
  2. Trace Vase Pattern onto music paper; cut out and fold on dotted lines.
  3. Cut tan paper, with a decorative edge on curved end, slightly smaller than folded paper. Insert tan paper inside folded paper.
  4. Cut black paper slightly larger than folded paper and glue onto background.
  5. Punch seven medium and one small heart from red paper.

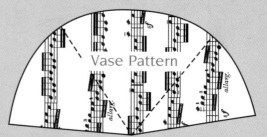

Vase Pattern

Enlarge 200%

6. Glue small heart onto seam of folded paper.
7. Cut out stems for heart flowers and glue onto black vase.
8. Glue medium hearts onto stems and background as shown on scrapbook page.
9. Glue folded paper onto black paper over flower stems.

● Large heart punch • Red paper scraps • Black uppercase sticker lettering:
1. Punch enough hearts for name plus one and glue hearts onto background. Note: *Place two hearts overlapping for one letter.*
2. Place letters on hearts.

Tip: Heart patterns can be made and traced onto red paper if you do not have access to heart punches.

Tip: You may want to have a scrapbook for each child of the family, which could be passed on to them so their spouse and children can see how they spent time as a child.

95

It's A Boy

Helen and Jack Wall
Maternity Wing

Labor Delivery
Ante Partum Testing

Neonatology
Nursery
Special Care Nursery
Maternity
Patient Rooms
Perinatal
High Risk Unit

It's a Boy

This can be a quick page that uses some great paper combinations. The papers consist of stripes, diagonals, and dots, with blue as the dominant color. You can add die-cuts and stickers using the same color combinations for the finishing touch. A combination of photos was used to tell the story.

★ Blue/white polka-dot patterned paper for background

★ Photos:
1. Crop photos as desired.

★ Blue/yellow/white striped and blue/purple/teal/yellow diagonal striped papers:
1. Cut papers slightly larger than photos and glue photos onto papers.
2. Glue photos onto background.

★ ⅛"-wide blue strip and baby-themed stickers:
1. Place blue strip on bottom of background. Place some of the stickers on center of strip.
2. Place remainder of stickers on background.

★ "It's A Boy," duck, and diaper pin die-cuts:
1. Glue die-cuts onto background.

> **Tip:** You may have seen patterned papers in the scrapbooking stores and wonder how to mix and match them. The key is to select patterned papers which have one or more common colors.

I LOVE THE DUCK!

I Love the Duck!

You may want to try taking a roll of black-and-white film on occasion and making a scrapbook page that is interesting and different. This was one of those "special shots" which calls for a page of its own, so it was enlarged and color copied to go on this special page.

- Black card stock and glossy black paper for background:
  1. Cut paper smaller than card stock and glue onto card stock.

- Oval template • Black-and-white photo:
  1. Enlarge to desired size and color copy photo.
  2. Trace an oval onto color copy and crop.

- Decorative-edged scissors • Med. gray card stock:
  1. Trace an oval ¼" larger than photo onto card stock and cut out with decorative edge. Glue color copy onto card stock.
  2. Glue color copy and card stock onto background.

- Decorative-edged scissors • Mickey Mouse punch • Med. gray card stock • Matte silver paper:
  1. Cut 1¼"-wide strip from card stock and paper. Punch out Mickey Mouse every 2". Note: *If you turn the paper over and punch out from the wrong side, Mickey will run both directions.*
  2. Cut circles and squares around punches with decorative edges.
  3. Glue punches onto background.

- Metallic silver sticker lettering • Opaque metallic silver medium-point pen:
  1. Place lettering on background.
  2. Draw dots around gray mat as shown on scrapbook page.
  3. Dot around bottom edge of lettering.

At the Cottage

The cottage is so much fun that everyone hates to go home! Remember those extended family traditions by taking lots of photos and making scrapbook pages that show the family members and their activities. This page includes candid and posed shots, along with a landscape shot of the beautiful lake.

▲ Camping motif patterned paper (2) for backgrounds • Removable tape:
   1. Lay card stock side by side and tape together on the back side.

▲ Circle template • Photo-safe pencil • Photos:
   1. Trace a circle onto one photo and crop.
   2. Crop remaining photos as desired.

▲ Blue and green papers:
   1. Cut green paper slightly larger than circle photo and glue photo onto green paper.
   2. Cut blue paper slightly larger than photo and green paper. Double-mat photo onto blue paper.
   3. Cut blue and green papers slightly larger than remaining photos and glue photos onto papers.
   4. Glue photos onto backgrounds.

▲ Moose die-cut:
   1. Glue moose onto background.

▲ Green medium-point marker • Oatmeal-flecked paper • Green upper- and lowercase sticker lettering:
   1. Cut paper into squares larger than lettering and place lettering on squares.
   2. Draw dash and dot border around outside edge of squares. Glue lettering onto backgrounds.
   3. Remove tape from background and cut down center between pages, separating any art that is glued onto both backgrounds.

our new baby

This is a beautiful piece of paper with a busy, overall pattern, which can be difficult to use as a background. When the background is treated with soft, tinted colors and gentle-styled photos, it makes a beautiful page. There is a certain "quietness" here because of the subject and the photos. Soft gold and peach papers surround the photos with some photos double-matted. Lettering and stickers were selected in the same soft, muted baby colors.

- Baby-themed patterned paper for background

- Oval template • Photo-safe pencil • Photos:
  1. Trace ovals onto two photos and crop.
  2. Crop remaining photos as desired.

- Birth announcement or hospital certificates:
  1. Crop as desired and glue onto background.

- Soft peach and soft gold papers • Black lowercase sticker lettering:
  1. Trace ovals slightly larger than oval photos and crop. Note: *Oval photos may be double-matted with both colors.*
  2. Cut papers slightly larger than remaining photos for matting. Glue photos onto papers.
  3. Glue photos onto background.
  4. Cut rectangles slightly larger than individual letters from soft gold paper. Place letters on rectangles.
  5. Glue letters onto background.

- Baby-themed stickers:
  1. Place stickers on background.

our new baby

Nom : *Taylar*

Prénoms : *Céline Alexis*

Née le : *5 octobre 1998*
à : *Neuilly-sur-Seine*

Nationalité : *Américaine*

Taille : *46 cm*

Poids : *2 kg 340*

Mes parents : *Stephanie et Sam Taylar*
Ma sœur : *Ashton*
Domicile : *9, boulevard du Château*
92200 Neuilly-sur-Seine, France

Chapter Five

Moving Along

Moving along to more detailed pages does not mean difficult, it means "more" in the way of stickers, pen work, lettering ideas, papers—well, you get the idea!

These pages will take a little more time because they are more detailed, but they will be well worth it.

A large number of children are playing soccer or other sports these days, so why not create a page with photos of your athlete and their team members. Combine the photos and soccer stickers with bright papers for contrast to make a creative page. Use this idea with baseball or softball stickers, or the swim team with fish or other related stickers.

● Blue card stock for background

● Photos:
  1. Crop photos as desired. Note: *One or more photos may be cropped long and narrow like a panoramic shot.*

● Soccer ball patterned and bright yellow papers:
  1. Cut soccer ball paper larger than individual photo and glue photo onto soccer paper.
  2. Cut yellow paper larger than soccer ball paper and photo and double-mat photo onto yellow paper.
  3. Cut yellow strip paper larger than team photo as shown on scrapbook page and frame photo onto yellow paper.
  4. Cut strip of soccer ball paper as shown on scrapbook page.
  5. Cut strip of yellow paper larger than soccer ball paper and glue soccer ball paper on yellow paper.
  6. Glue photos and soccer ball paper onto background.

- Black/white checkered patterned and lime green paper scraps • Black upper case lettering:
  1. Cut checkered paper in squares larger than letters and place letters on paper.
  2. Cut green paper wider than checkered paper and glue checkered paper onto green paper.

3. Glue lettering onto background in tumbled fashion.

- Soccer stickers • Black pen (optional):
  1. Place stickers on background.
  Option: Write child's name and age on scrapbook page.

105

Céline

Usually babies are photographed
too far away to see their features
and beautiful skin, so try shooting
close-ups to create your baby scrapbook page.

✦ Pink parchment paper for background

✦ Oval templates • Photo-safe pencil • Photos:
    1. Trace ovals onto some photos and crop.
    2. Crop remaining photos as desired.

✦ Gold parchment paper:
    1. Cut paper slightly larger than photos and
    glue photos onto paper.
    2. Glue photos onto background.

✦ Floral, initial sticker lettering:
    1. Place lettering on page. *Note: Extra letters
    may be applied to fill up void spaces.*

✦ Opaque silver pen:
    1. Draw scroll and dot designs around matted
    photos and on background.

Summer Memories

These are favorite scrapbook pages, because they hold precious memories. Maybe knowing that this town is where "The Sound of Music" was filmed also has something to do with it. The play money was purchased in a toy store in this city, music-themed paper was cut up, and one of our favorite photos was enlarged.

This layout can be used for any vacation, whether it is in Europe, Asia, Boston, Seattle, or just a few hours away from home. Start with some interesting shots of popular landmarks, always remembering to look for those candid shots that tell the story and keep the memories alive. Watch for unusual items from drug stores, travel agencies, and hotel lobbies you can place on scrapbook pages. It is important to remember that scrapbook pages and the materials placed on them should be of archival quality.

Dk. green card stock for backgrounds
• Removable tape:
1. Lay card stock side by side and tape together on the back side.

▶ Music-themed paper:
1. Cut paper into desired sizes and glue onto backgrounds.

▶ Photos:
1. Crop photos as desired.

▶ Pale gray marbled paper • Play paper money • Buffering spray:
1. Spray paper money with buffering spray, if necessary.
2. Cut paper slightly larger than photos and glue photos onto paper.
3. Glue photos and paper onto backgrounds.

▶ Coins • Black card stock and gold paper scraps • Decorative-edged scissors • Double-sided tape runner • Plastic page protector:
1. Cut 2" x 3" rectangle from card stock.
2. Cut gold paper slightly smaller than card stock with decorative edges and glue onto card stock.
3. Cut 5" x 7" rectangle from page protector.
4. Place matted paper and card stock right side down onto center of plastic. Pull edges up tight lengthwise and secure with double-sided tape runner. Fold one end over and secure.

5. Slip coins into front side of packet and secure remaining end in back. Glue coins onto background.

▶ Sticker lettering • Musical note stickers:
1. Place lettering on background.
2. Place stickers on background.
3. Remove tape from background and cut down center between pages, separating any art that is glued onto both backgrounds.

BEACH TRIP

There is something special about taking a picnic lunch and spending the day on the beach. Take lots of photos such as baby on the blanket, in mommy's and daddy's arms, as well as an afternoon "snooze" under the beach umbrella to record the activities of the day.

* Pale aqua card stock (2) for backgrounds:
   1. Lay card stock side by side and tape together on the back side.

* Med. blue and turquoise papers • Wave decorative-edged ruler:
   1. Trace wave edge onto med. blue paper and cut out.
   2. Trace wave edge onto turquoise paper and cut out.
   3. Glue blue paper onto backgrounds, matching edges where pages meet.

110

* Turquoise upper-case sticker lettering:
    1. Place lettering on backgrounds.

* Blue and aqua medium-point markers:
    1. Draw bubbles coming from the sea animals on backgrounds.
    2. Remove tape from background and cut down center between pages, separating any art that is glued onto both backgrounds.

4. Glue turquoise paper lower than blue paper, matching edges where pages meet.

* Circle and oval templates • Round corner punch • Photo-safe pencil • Photos:
    1. Trace circles and ovals onto some photos and crop.
    2. Crop remaining photos in squares and punch corners.

* Sea horse, fish, dolphin, octopus, and sun die-cuts:
    1. Glue photos and die-cuts onto backgrounds.

Wrigley Field

Adapt this style of layout to any sports event that you or your family attends. The tickets, popcorn, pretzels, and baseball stickers were purchased at the scrapbook store. The bats and giant baseball were cut from patterned papers, while the pennants were cut from white paper.

Option: Cut blue paper larger than one or more photos and glue photos onto paper.

● Large baseball patterned paper:
  1. Cut out baseball.
  2. Glue photos and baseball onto backgrounds.

● Baseball bat patterned and white papers • Baseball, popcorn, pretzel, and ticket stickers • Blue and red medium-point pens:
  1. Cut out baseball bats and glue onto background. *Note: The bats were cut out individually and glued onto the background in a grouping.*
  2. Place stickers on background.
  3. Cut out pennants and glue onto background.
  4. Draw red border around edge of pennant and add blue text in center of pennant.
  5. Remove tape from background and cut down center between pages, separating any art that is glued onto both backgrounds.

● Red/white grid patterned paper for backgrounds • Removable tape:
  1. Lay card stock side by side and tape together on the back side.

● Photos:
  1. Crop photos as desired.

● ¼"-wide blue strip stickers • Blue paper (optional):
  1. Place a strip on one straight edge of each photo.

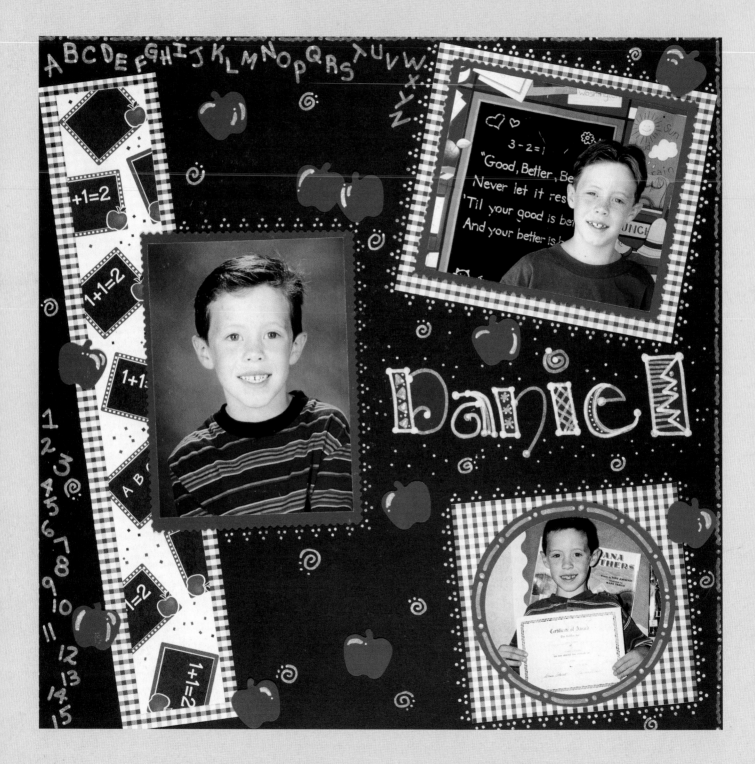

1+1=2 Daniel 2+2=4

Acknowledge a child's academic achievement with their very own scrap-book page. Even if they do not have any extra special accomplishments, make a page each year to let them feel pride and achievement in learning. This page uses a few apple punches, but relies on an opaque white pen for the decorative elements.

■ Black card stock for background

■ Circle template • Photo-safe pencil • Photos:
  1. Trace a circle onto one photo and crop.
  2. Crop remaining photos as desired.

■ Apple punch • Decorative-edged scissors • Red card stock:
  1. Cut one red card stock circle ¼" larger than circle photo. Glue photo onto card stock.
  2. Cut red card stock larger than remaining photos with decorative edges. Glue photos onto card stock.
  3. Punch eight to ten apples from card stock.

■ School-themed and black/white gingham papers:
  1. Cut gingham paper square larger than red circle. Double-mat photo onto gingham paper.
  2. Cut gingham paper larger than one photo. Double-mat photo onto paper.
  3. Cut 1½"–2" strip of black/white gingham paper.
  4. Cut strip ¼" larger than school-themed paper. Glue school-themed paper onto gingham paper.
  5. Glue paper strip, photos, and apples onto background.

■ Pencil • Opaque white pen • White sticker lettering (optional):
  1. Draw white numbers, alphabets, swirls, dots, and borders on background as shown on scrapbook page.
  2. Draw white markings on apples.
  3. Lightly pencil name on background and trace over name with white.
  Note: *Practice name on a separate sheet of paper.*
  Option: *White sticker lettering may be used if you feel uncomfortable writing on the background.*

EASTER EGG

Who can resist a baby or child popping out of an "Easter" egg? The background paper has a fresh spring-like color of yellow stripes.

◆ Egg Pattern:
1. Enlarge Egg Pattern 200% and photocopy onto white card stock.
2. Cut egg from card stock for egg template.
3. Cut along jagged edges in center of egg for top and bottom eggshell pattern.

◆ Yellow/white striped patterned paper for background

◆ Photo • Photo-safe pencil:
1. Place egg template on photo and trace egg. Crop photo and glue onto background.

◆ Lavender paper • Segmented tape • Easter grass:
1. Trace eggshell patterns onto paper and cut out.
2. Apply tape to back side of bottom eggshell. Line up bottom edge of eggshell with photo edge and press.
3. Place small amount of Easter grass in eggshell and press, adding extra tape where necessary.
4. Repeat with top eggshell.

◆ Silver metallic medium-point pen:
1. Outline jagged edges of eggshells.
2. Draw decorative border on top and bottom of page.

◆ EASTER die-cut:
1. Glue die-cut onto page.

◆ Rabbit punch • Pink paper:
1. Punch seven rabbits from paper and glue onto background.

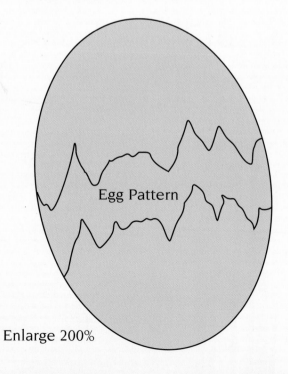

Egg Pattern

Enlarge 200%

116

◆ Diamond punch
• Cloud patterned paper:
  1. Punch nineteen diamonds from paper and glue onto eggshells.

◆ Circle punch • Pale green paper:
  1. Punch fourteen circles from paper and glue onto eggshells.

◆ Opaque white pen:
  1. Dot an eye on each rabbit.
  2. Draw and color a circle in the center of punched circles.
  3. Dot eggshell with decorative dots.

◆ Butterflies, eggs, and flower stickers:
  1. Place butterflies on die-cut.
  2. Place flowers on egg shells.
  3. Place eggs tumbling down the sides of background.

Tip: When selecting the photo for this page, a child dressed in light pastel or white clothing will look best.

Tip:
Tiny flower stickers can be cut from an arch or wreath sticker. Save the greenery for use on another scrapbook page.

Halloween

Holiday theme pages are always fun to do, and each holiday has its own traditional colors and motifs to design around. The vibrancy of colors and the whimsical stickers tell the story of this Halloween party for preschoolers.

★ White card stock (2) for backgrounds:
   1. Lay card stock side by side and tape together on the back side.

★ Green and yellow medium-point markers:
   1. Draw two green parallel lines on sides and bottom of backgrounds as shown on scrapbook pages.
   2. Draw one wavy line through green lines.

★ Circle and oval templates • Photo-safe pencil • Photos:
   1. Trace circles and ovals onto photos and crop.

★ Bright orange, orange, and yellow papers:
   1. Cut papers larger than photos and glue photos onto papers.

2. Double-mat two to three photos.
3. Glue photos onto background.

★ "Halloween" die-cut • Halloween theme and star stickers:
1. Glue die-cut onto background.
2. Place stickers on backgrounds.

★ Orange and red medium-point markers:
1. Randomly dot groups of four orange dots with a red dot in the middle on backgrounds.
2. Remove tape from background and cut down center between pages, separating any art that is glued onto both backgrounds.

Tip: Purchase supplies associated with holidays when you see them, because chances are you will wish you had later on.

Thanksgiving

The annual gathering of Thanksgiving is great fun with lots of turkey and family inter-action, especially in the case of the children, whether they are playing with cousins or interacting with the adults. Page layout consists of photos, die-cuts, and pen-drawn designs.

◆ Oatmeal-flecked paper:
   1. Cut paper into rectangle shapes and glue onto background.
   2. Glue photos onto background.

◆ Black fine-point, dk. green medium-point, and brown medium-point markers:
   1. Draw border across top edge of page and around photos as shown on scrapbook page.

◆ Brown and green self-adhesive leaf and acorn die-cuts:
   1. Place leaves and acorns on backgrounds.

◆ Lt. gold card stock (2) for backgrounds:
   1. Lay card stock side by side and tape together on the back side.

◆ Oval template • Photo-safe pencil • Photos:
   1. Trace an oval onto one photo and crop.
   2. Crop remaining photos.

◆ Dk. green sticker lettering • Black fine-tip pen:
   1. Place lettering on background and accent with black dots as shown on scrapbook page.
   2. Remove tape from background and cut down center between pages, separating any art that is glued onto both backgrounds.

First Train Ride

Make scrapbook pages that include "firsts," such as a train ride, pony ride, the slide at the park, or any other firsts. In this case, the train picture is a postcard picked up at the train station.

The photos are surrounded with different shades of green papers, and the backgrounds are pen-dotted. Using one color, such as green, can be very effective when used in a variety of tones and shades.

▼ White card stock (2) for backgrounds
  • Removable tape:
  1. Lay card stock side by side and tape together on the back side.

▼ Circle, oval, and octagon templates
  • Photo-safe pencil
  • Photos:
  1. Trace a circle onto one photo and crop.
  2. Trace an octagon onto one photo and crop.
  3. Trace ovals onto two to three photos and crop.
  4. Crop remaining photos as desired.

▼ Lime green medium-point marker:
    1. Draw single-line border ¼" from background edge.

▼ Leaf green, lt. green, lime green, and med. green papers:
    1. Cut papers larger than photos and glue photos onto papers.
    2. Glue photos onto backgrounds.

▼ Shamrock die-cut
    • Shamrock stickers
    • Coordinating sticker lettering:
    1. Glue die-cuts onto background.
    2. Place stickers and lettering on background.

▼ Green and black medium-point markers:
    1. Decorate backgrounds with lines and dots.
    2. Remove tape from background and cut down center between pages, separating any art that is glued onto both backgrounds.

at the park with cousins

Pole Patterns

This is a fun page to do because of the opportunity for great photos. The play equipment and children are in bright primary colors and photos were shot close up and at a distance. Photos were taken of the children on the play equipment so that the equipment shapes could be reproduced on the page. Remember to include the sandpile with a sand castle, and of course, a few ladybug and kite stickers.

■ Green card stock (2) for backgrounds • Removable tape:
  1. Lay card stock side by side and tape together on the back side.

■ Circle and oval templates • Photo-safe pencil • Photos:
  1. Trace a circle onto one photo and crop.
  2. Trace ovals onto two photos and crop.
  3. Crop remaining photos as desired.

■ Oatmeal-flecked patterned, and blue and yellow papers • Pole, Roof, and Slide Patterns:

1. Cut yellow ovals slightly larger than photos and glue photos onto paper.

2. Cut blue paper with a wavy edge slightly larger than circle photo and glue photo onto blue paper.

3. Enlarge as desired and photocopy Pole patterns on page 124, and Roof and Slide Patterns onto white card stock and cut out.

4. Trace Pole Patterns onto blue paper and cut out.

5. Trace Roof Pattern onto yellow paper and cut out.

6. Glue playground equipment to backgrounds to accommodate cropped photos.

7. Cut oatmeal paper into an irregular shape for sandpile and glue onto background.

8. Glue photos onto background as desired.

■ Yellow lowercase sticker lettering
• Caterpillar, kites, and ladybug stickers:

1. Place sticker lettering on background.

2. Place stickers on background.

3. Remove tape from background and cut down center between pages, separating any art that is glued onto both backgrounds.

park with cousins

Slide
Pattern

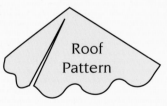

Roof
Pattern

Best Friends

Since pets are often an important part of the family, it is only natural to make scrapbook pages portraying these special family friends. Various family members and their pet dogs are included on this page along with theme stickers.

Tan card stock for background

♥ Circle and oval templates • Photo-safe pencil • Photos:
  1. Trace circle onto one photo and crop.
  2. Trace oval onto one photo and crop.
  3. Crop remaining photos as desired.

♥ Green/red plaid patterned paper:
  1. Cut paper slightly larger than photos and glue photos onto background.

Dog-themed stickers:
  1. Place stickers on background as desired.

Index

Metric Equivalency Chart

mm–millimetres   cm–centimetres
inches to millimetres and centimetres

inches	mm	cm	inches	cm	inches	cm
⅛	3	0.3	9	22.9	30	76.2
¼	6	0.6	10	25.4	31	78.7
⅜	10	1.0	11	27.9	32	81.3
½	13	1.3	12	30.5	33	83.8
⅝	16	1.6	13	33.0	34	86.4
¾	19	1.9	14	35.6	35	88.9
⅞	22	2.2	15	38.1	36	91.4
1	25	2.5	16	40.6	37	94.0
1¼	32	3.2	17	43.2	38	96.5
1½	38	3.8	18	45.7	39	99.1
1¾	44	4.4	19	48.3	40	101.6
2	51	5.1	20	50.8	41	104.1
2½	64	6.4	21	53.3	42	106.7
3	76	7.6	22	55.9	43	109.2
3½	89	8.9	23	58.4	44	111.8
4	102	10.2	24	61.0	45	114.3
4½	114	11.4	25	63.5	46	116.8
5	127	12.7	26	66.0	47	119.4
6	152	15.2	27	68.6	48	121.9
7	178	17.8	28	71.1	49	124.5
8	203	20.3	29	73.7	50	127.0